Can God See Me?

written by JoDee McConnaughhay
illustrated by Max Kolding

Thank you Wendy, Jamie, April, Chris, and the FCCF youth leaders for your godly example—and for "watching over" my children.

08 07 06 05 04   9 8 7 6

ISBN 0-7847-1104-6

Standard
PUBLISHING
CINCINNATI, OHIO

Matthew looked up at the stars. So many. So far away. Matthew wondered, "Is God farther than the stars? Can God see me from so far?"

Grandpa was older and smarter than Matthew. Maybe he would know. And besides . . .

Grandpa was right there.
"Grandpa?" said Matthew.
"Yes?" Grandpa answered.

"Is God farther than the stars? I just
want to know. Can he see me here—
way down below?"

"The Bible tells us 'The Lord watches
over all who love him,' " Grandpa said.
"You're never too far for God to see you."

"Inside our dark tent, can God see me? How?
Tell me, please, Grandpa. I want to know now."

" 'The Lord watches over all who love him,' "
Grandpa said. "You can't hide from God—
even in the dark."

"But when I'm in a crowd, I feel so small.
Can God tell it's me—not Patti or Paul?"

" 'The Lord watches over all who love him,' "
Grandpa said. "He knows it's you. He knows
your name."

"What if I stay in a hospital bed? Will God know I'm there, not home instead?"

" 'The Lord watches over all who love him,' "
Grandpa said. "God sees each time you hurt or cry;
he knows what you need to get well."

"What if I lived in an igloo of ice?
Could God see me there, call my name
once or twice?"

" 'The Lord watches over all who love him,' "
Grandpa said. "That means God sees you
wherever you are."

"Even in a submarine, deep in the sea?
Under the water, can God still see me?"

" 'The Lord watches over all who love him,' "
Grandpa said. "And God made the oceans—
so he'd know where to find you."

"If I'm in a spaceship way past the moon,
would I be closer to God than I am in my room?"

"Matthew," Grandpa said. "God is everywhere. He's as close as our hearts. He's as near as a prayer."

Matthew stared at the sky. Then, opening his arms as wide as could be, he said, " 'The Lord watches over all who love him'—and that means ME!"

Suggestion to Parent

As your child becomes familiar with the story, encourage him or her to repeat the Scripture phrase with you each time it appears. Then, try letting your child *finish* the Scripture phrase each time it appears. Before long, your child will have memorized the verse!

"The Lord watches over all who love him."
—*Psalm 145:20*